The E-mail

by
Linda Kita-Bradley

Grass Roots Press

The E-mail is published by

Grass Roots Press, a division of Literacy Services of Canada Ltd.
Phone: 1-888-303-3213
Website: www.grassrootsbooks.net

ACKNOWLEDGMENTS

We acknowledge the financial support of the Government of Canada through the Canada Book Fund (CBF) for our publishing activities.

Produced with the assistance of the Government of Alberta, Alberta Multimedia Development Fund.

Government of Alberta ■

Editor: Dr. Pat Campbell
Photography: Grass Roots Press
Book design: Lara Minja, Lime Design Inc.

Library and Archives Canada Cataloguing in Publication

Kita-Bradley, Linda, 1958–
    The e-mail / Linda Kita-Bradley.

ISBN 978–1–926583–92–1

    1. Readers for new literates.   2. Readers—Privacy.   I. Title.

PE1126.N43K58253 2012   428.6'2   C2012–902999–8

Printed in Canada

This is Pat and Len.

Pat and Len live together.

Sometimes Pat and Len fight.

Most days they get along.

Len is a cab driver.

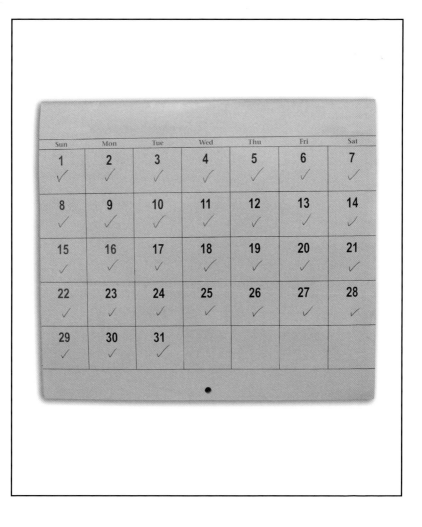

He works every day.

Sometimes Len works late.

So he calls Pat.

Sometimes Len does not call.

One night, Pat calls Len.
Len does not answer.

They have a fight.

Pat worries.

Can she trust Len?

The next day, Len goes to work.

"Oh! Look!" says Pat.
"Len's phone."

Pat stares at the phone.

Pat stares and stares.

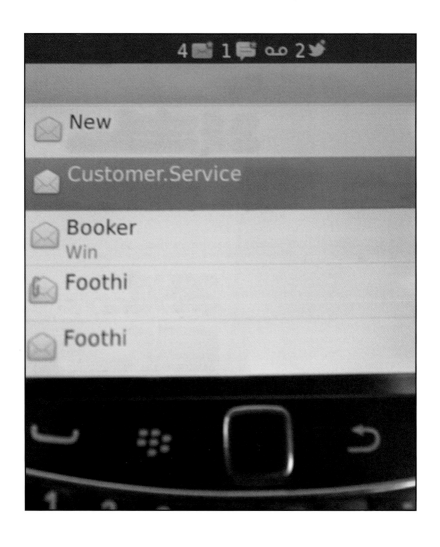

Len's e-mail is open.

Should she read Len's e-mail?

Why not?

Len has nothing to hide.

Pat picks up the phone.